Contents

The meaning of Thanksgiving

LATE AUTUMN! THE AIR TURNS CRISP, and it grows dark earlier. In the United States and Canada, one source of light in the time before Christmas is Thanksgiving.

As the leaves on the trees in Vermont, USA, change colour, thoughts turn to Thanksgiving.

EARLY HARVEST FESTIVALS

The first Thanksgivings that were celebrated in the United States were harvest festivals. All over the world, such festivals have been held from the earliest times. On these days people gathered to give thanks that they had enough food for the coming year. The American Thanksgiving Day probably grew out of harvest festivals that English colonists had seen before going to America. In both America and Canada, Thanksgiving still takes place in late autumn, after the crops have been harvested. On this day, which is now an official holiday, people give thanks for the blessings of the past year.

The flavours of the very first Thanksgiving feasts can be tasted today in Massachusetts, USA.

6

THANKSGIVING

AND OTHER HARVEST FESTIVALS

Evans Brothers Limited

Published by Evans Brothers Limited
2A Portman Mansions
Chiltern Street
London WIM 1LE

British Library Cataloguing in Publication data.

Miller, Marilyn
   Thanksgiving. – (A world of festivals)
   1. Thanksgiving Day – Juvenile literature
   I. Title
   394.2 649

ISBN 0 237 51803 1

First published 1998

Printed in Spain by G.Z. Printek

ACKNOWLEDGEMENTS

Editor: Su Swallow
Design: Raynor Design
Production: Jenny Mulvanny

The author and Publishers would like to thank the
following for permission to reproduce photographs:

Cover Trip/S Grant
Title page Pamela Hamilton/Image Bank

page 6 (top) Simon Harris/Robert Harding Picture
Library (bottom) Zefa Pictures **page 7** Robert
Harding Picture Library **page 8** (top right) Getty
Images (bottom left) Trip/Viesti **page 9** Private
Collection/Bridgeman Art Library **page 10**
Historical Society of Pennsylvania, USA/Bridgeman
Art Library **page 11** (top right) National Portrait
Gallery, Smithsonian Institute/Bridgeman Art Library
(bottom left) Trip/Peter Bennett, Viesti **page 12** (top
left) Trip/ Viesti (bottom left) Hulton Getty Images
page 13 Trip/Viesti **page 14** (top left) Trip/Ginny
Ganong Nichols, Viesti (main image) Private
Collection/Bridgeman Art Library **page 15** (top)
R Bamber (bottom left) Tony Stone (bottom right)
Tony Stone **page 16** (left) Kenneth Redding/Image
Bank (right) Zefa Pictures **page 17** (top) Luis
Castaneda/Image Bank (bottom) Rob Van
Petten/Image Bank **page 18** (left) Trip/Viesti (right)
Trip/Viesti **page 19** (top) Pamela Hamilton/Image
Bank (bottom) Trip/Viesti **page 20** (top) Craig
Aurness/Robert Harding Picture Library (bottom)
Ron Watts/Robert Harding Picture Library **page 21**
(top) Robert Estall Photo Library (bottom) Alain
Evrard/Robert Harding Picture Library **page 22**
(top) Trip/Viesti (bottom) Trip/Viesti **page 23**
Trip/Viesti **page 24** (left) Panos Pictures (right) Jon
Spaull/Panos Pictures **page 25** Christine Osborne
Pictures **page 26/27** Trip/H Rogers **page 28 and 29**
Anthony King/Medimage

FAMILIES GATHER TOGETHER

Thanksgiving is traditionally a family day, celebrated with big turkey dinners and happy reunions. Children especially love this holiday filled with delicious food. In the days before Thanksgiving, airports and roads are jammed as family members travel to be together. Friends are often invited to share the holiday dinner. Although this joyful holiday is associated with the good smells of cooking and baking, it has a serious side. For Thanksgiving is also a day for church services and prayer.

Turkey takes pride of place on most Thanksgiving tables!

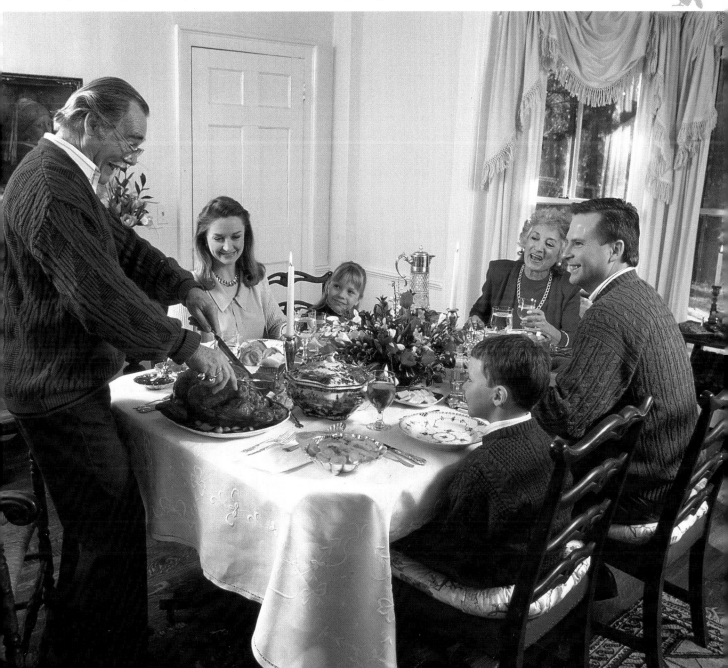

The first Thanksgiving in America

THE VERY FIRST THANKS-GIVING was celebrated by thirty-eight English settlers after they arrived at Berkeley Plantation on the James River in Virginia, in America.

At the first Thanksgiving, the English Pilgrims offered prayers of thanks for their safe arrival in America.

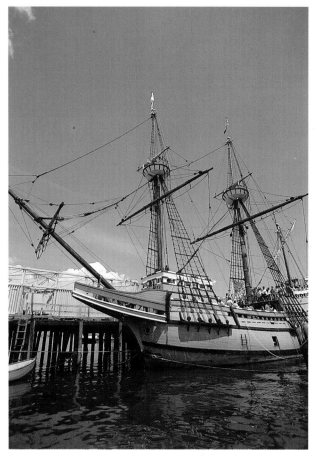

A replica of the *Mayflower*, which sailed from Plymouth, in England, to America in 1620

THE PILGRIMS CELEBRATE IN NEW ENGLAND

On this first Thanksgiving, the settlers prayed but did not feast. But a bigger celebration which is often mistakenly believed to be the first Thanksgiving took place in New England.

In 1620, 102 English settlers on the sailing ship *Mayflower* landed at what is now Plymouth, Massachusetts, in New England, USA. The place where they settled was named the Plimouth Plantation.

An artist painted this picture of the first Thanksgiving feast nearly 300 years after the event.

A harsh winter, hunger, and sickness killed about half of the settlers during that first year. By the summer of 1621, the lives of the surviving Pilgrims, as they were called, had greatly improved. Expecting a good corn harvest, Governor William Bradford arranged a harvest festival for the Pilgrims to rejoice together.

The Pilgrims celebrated for three days. The men shot turkeys, geese, ducks, and deer. The women cooked and prepared the food. Other foods were smoked eel, clams, herbs and rye bread. About ninety Massachuset Indians were invited to share the feast. They brought five deer to add to the meal. There were games of skill and chance, and target-shooting with guns and bows and arrows. The Indians showed off some of their dances and Captain Miles Standish inspected his troops. It was a day to be remembered for everyone!

9

🦃 A public holiday 🦃

THE OTHER AMERICAN COLONIES LIKED the Pilgrim custom of celebrating a day of thanksgiving for good harvests. So they began celebrating this day too.

TWO SEPARATE THANKSGIVINGS

The Americans had other reasons to be happy. During the American War of Independence (1775–1783), they set aside eight days in thanks for their military victories against the British. After the War, General George Washington became the first president. In 1789, he named November 26 as a day of national thanksgiving. But during the same year, church leaders set aside the first Thursday in November as a day to give thanks. So Americans had at least two separate Thanksgiving days!

The Battle of Princeton, where General Washington led his troops to victory against the British in 1777.

A PRESIDENT DECIDES THE DATE

Different states also celebrated Thanksgiving on different days. The editor of a popular women's magazine, Sarah Josepha Hale, decided to do something about the confusion. For more than thirty years she asked American presidents to make Thanksgiving Day a national holiday. Finally, in 1863, President Abraham Lincoln ordered that the last Thursday in November should be observed as a special day of national thanksgiving.

It was Abraham Lincoln who finally fixed the date for Thanksgiving.

ONE THANKSGIVING FOR EVERYONE

In 1939, President Franklin Roosevelt set the date for Thanksgiving one week earlier. He wanted to add another shopping week before Christmas. But some states kept the old date for Thanksgiving. So two years later, Congress changed Thanksgiving back to the fourth Thursday of November and made it a public holiday.

Canadians celebrate Thanksgiving, too. Their Thanksgiving Day falls on the second Monday in October.

A shop in New York, ready for Christmas. Americans celebrate two important festivals at the end of the year.

11

Bring on the parade!

PARADES HAVE LONG BEEN A PART of the Thanksgiving celebrations. The biggest Thanksgiving spectacle of all is in New York City. Millions of people watch a fantastic parade on television. It is organised by Macy's, the world's largest department store.

DRESSING UP!

Macy's' Thanksgiving Parade started in the 1920s. Many of Macy's' workers were new immigrants from countries in Europe. These workers had happy memories of holiday festivals in Europe. So they decided to hold a public celebration on Thanksgiving. What better way to share in the holiday spirit than a grand parade? Marchers dressed as cowboys and cowgirls, knights in armour, giants and clowns. There were floats, bands, and twenty-five animals borrowed from the zoo. The first parade was a great success.

GIANT BALLOONS

The wild animals in the parade frightened some of the children watching. So animal balloons were put in their place. The giant balloons are inflated with an air-and-helium mixture and float high above the crowd. Giant balloons such as Dino the Dinosaur, Dudley the Dragon, Sonic the Hedgehog and other popular characters mingle with oddities such as a 10-metre ice cream cone! Each year the parade ends with the arrival at Macy's of Santa Claus on his own float. His arrival marks the start of the Christmas season. Bands from high schools all over the country march in the parade.

Children wrapped up against the cold watch the Macy's parade in 1961.

More turkey, please!

I N THE UNITED STATES AND CANADA, Thanksgiving would not be Thanksgiving without turkey. For their Thanksgiving the Pilgrims feasted on wild turkeys cooked over an outdoor fire. They had hunted the turkeys in the surrounding woods.

An American artist's painting of a Thanksgiving turkey shoot

TURKEYS ON THE FARM

Today the turkeys on most Thanksgiving tables are White Hollands, whose plumage is all white. White Holland turkeys are raised on farms, mostly in fenced fields or pens. Farm turkeys have larger heads than wild turkeys. But wild turkeys can do something that farm turkeys cannot do. Wild turkeys can fly!

14

THE TURKEY'S IN THE OVEN

On the holiday morning kitchens fill with delicious smells of turkey roasting and pies baking in the oven. For many North Americans, Thanksgiving is their favourite 'food holiday'.

Big birds like turkeys need a lot of time to roast. Even small turkeys take about three hours to cook. The largest turkeys can weigh 11 kilograms and need about five hours to be done. If the turkeys are filled with stuffing, they are roasted a little longer. Turkey is traditionally served with mashed potatoes, squash (like marrow) and, especially, cranberry sauce.

Before everyone eats, a prayer is usually said at the table. There is no special Thanksgiving prayer, but in their prayers people give thanks for the blessings of the past year.

ALL THE PIES YOU CAN EAT

On Thanksgiving people usually eat until they are so full that they cannot

Thanksgiving turkey would not be the same without the cranberry sauce!

take one more bite! But before that happens, they leave a little space for Thanksgiving pies, made of fruit or mincemeat. But the traditional Thanksgiving pie is pumpkin pie. The Pilgrims learned about pumpkins from the Indians. They filled the pumpkin shell with milk, sugar and spice. Then they baked it in the fireplace. Today pumpkin pie is made with a pastry crust.

A feast for everyone, from oysters and turkey (left) to pumpkin pie (below)

Touchdown!

SINCE THE FIRST PILGRIM THANKSGIVING, Americans have loved to fill the day with holiday fun. In some parts of the country, young men used to light bonfires on the tops of hills. In New York City it was the custom before World War II for people to picnic in parks and then dance until dawn at grand balls.

Lining up to play. American football (left) and marching bands (below) are a traditional part of the Thanksgiving celebrations.

FOOTBALL IN NEW YORK CITY

Perhaps the activity that has become most associated with Thanksgiving is football. By the early 1890s, New York City was the site for the annual Thanksgiving Championship game between the two best college teams. As many as 40,000 people watched the game. Wearing their most elegant clothes and jewellery, the wealthiest spectators watched from special boxes.

OLD RIVALS

Some college football teams play each other every Thanksgiving. Since 1894, the University of Texas has played Texas A & M every Thanksgiving. The University of Texas has won sixty-six of these games! Other college teams have played against each other during the holiday since the 1950s. These games used to be on the holiday Thursday. But now most of the Thanksgiving college football games are played on the Saturday of the holiday weekend. College players are not the only ones on the football field during the holiday. High school football teams also play against their

Every team looks to its cheerleaders – and its mascot – to help them win, especially at Thanksgiving.

local rivals during the holiday. At the end of each of these games, the winning team often receives a trophy.

The winning team will enjoy this Thanksgiving even more!

17

🦃 A special Thanksgiving 🦃

THANKSGIVING IN PLYMOUTH, Massachusetts, where the first English Pilgrims landed, is very special. Every year thousands of visitors come to share in the holiday events.

FIFTY-ONE PILGRIMS

On Thanksgiving morning, excited crowds line the street to watch the march from Plymouth Rock to church. Each of the fifty-one costumed marchers represents one of the men, women and children who survived the first winter in the Plimouth Plantation colony (see page 8). Inside the church, worshippers sing psalms from the Book of Psalms in the Bible. The psalms praise God and thank him for his goodness. They are the same psalms that the Pilgrims sang.

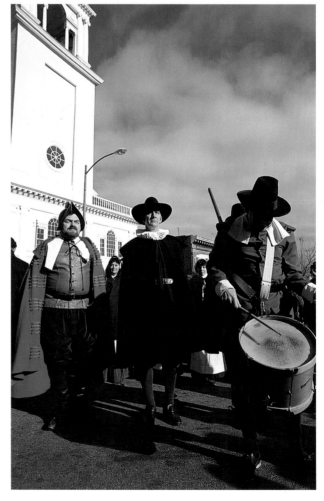

1990s 'Pilgrims' in Plymouth, Massachusetts relive the Thanksgiving of more than 350 years ago.

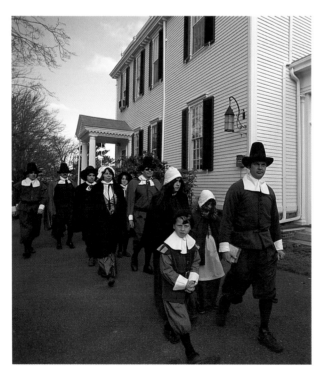

A TON OF TURKEY

Afterwards, Thanksgiving dinner is served to the public inside Memorial Hall. This dinner is based on the first Pilgrim holiday meal. It is served not once, but four times in a row, so that many people can eat. By the end, they have eaten about 450 kilograms of turkey! The dinner ends with Indian pudding, made with maize flour and sweetened with sugar and treacle.

LIVING HISTORY

Today, Plimouth Plantation is an outdoor museum – open from April to November – which recreates the life of a Pilgrim village of 1627. Actors in costume perform many of the original Pilgrim activities, such as planting crops.

The story of Thanksgiving is told on a greetings card.

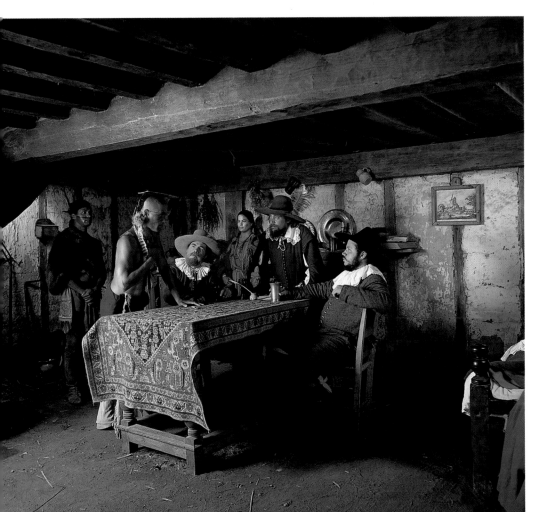

The meeting of Pilgrims and Indians is re-enacted at the Plimouth Plantation Museum.

19

Northern lights

IN CANADA, Thanksgiving is a family holiday, just as it is in the United States. But America's northern neighbour gets more than one month headstart on the festivities. Canadians celebrate their Thanksgiving in October.

THE WAR IS OVER!

In 1763 British colonists in Canada had much to cheer about. The Seven Years War between England and France, which had begun in 1756, was finally over. At the end of the war, France handed Canada over to England. The people of Halifax, Nova

Thanksgiving in Canada is an opportunity to give thanks for the harvest (above). It is also the time to close up the lakeside log cabins for the winter (below).

Scotia, decided to mark this happy event by a day of Thanksgiving. Over the years the custom spread to other parts of Canada. The holiday was not a religious holiday but a national day of giving thanks for the blessings of the past year.

In 1957 Parliament said that people all over Canada should celebrate Thanksgiving on the same day, the second Monday in October. And that is what they have done ever since.

Thanksgiving celebrations in Canada are very like those in America. But French Canadians may have ham or lamb instead of turkey, and in the country you might find *la tourtière*, a pastry pie of many layers filled with potatoes, rabbit or hare and partridge or pheasant!

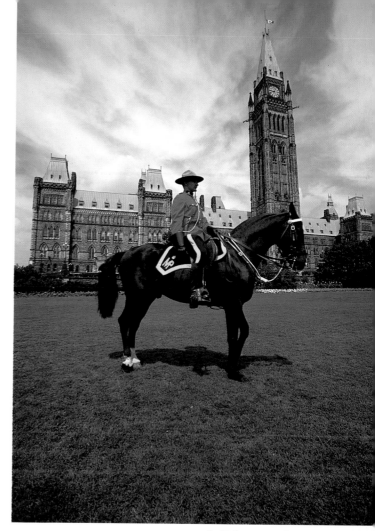

A 'Mountie' stands guard in front of Canada's Parliament buildings in Ottawa.

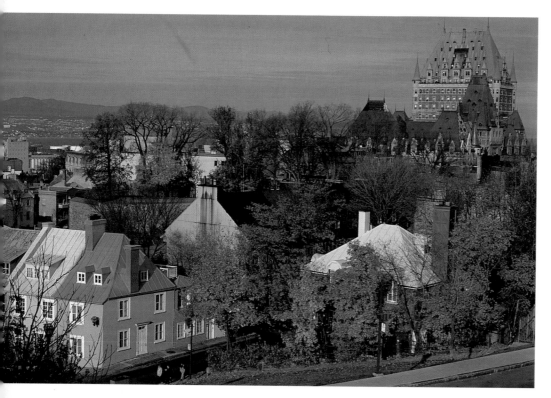

A French-style castle, now a hotel, dominates the city of Quebec, in the part of Canada that was once French.

21

Thanksgiving in Europe

Flowers and ribbons fit for any festival!

O THER COUNTRIES IN THE WORLD have special days for giving thanks in the autumn. In the Czech Republic, October 28 is a day of thanksgiving. On this day, people go to church to give thanks for the harvest. The next day they dance and feast.

TWO DAYS TO CELEBRATE!

The Czechs have two harvest celebrations. The church part of the holiday is called *Posviceni*. The joyous day of dancing and feasting, which follows, is called *Obzinky*. After the harvest is completed, farm workers make wreaths of rye, wild flowers, straw, or ears of wheat. These wreaths are placed on the heads of the prettiest

Children dance in traditional Czech costume – this time in Texas, USA!

girls. Next, everyone makes their way to the owner of the land, to present him with a wreath. Then he invites the farm workers to dance and feast. And what happens to the wreath? The landowner usually saves it in a place of honour until the next harvest.

A SPECIAL TREAT!

Guests at the feast are usually served with roast goose and roast pig. Many people also love to eat *sauerkraut* – a dish of shredded, pickled cabbage. And there is another special treat, a cake called *Kolache*. These cakes are filled with jam, sweetened cottage cheese, or poppy seeds. Delicious!

Making *Kolache* is a serious business – but eating them is great!

Festivals in Africa

IN SIERRA LEONE, IN AFRICA, Thanksgiving can be celebrated at any time during the year. During this day people of every religion sit down at a feast. They thank the spirits of their dead ancestors for all the good things that have happened.

INVITATION TO THE FEAST

The people of Sierra Leone call their Thanksgiving feast, the *Awoojoh*. The day begins with a family visit to the graves of ancestors. There, the family invite the dead to the feast.

Lost in thought. Thanksgiving festivals everywhere are a time to remember the good things that have happened.

Bright cottons fit for any feast day

Afterwards, the family returns home. Inside they settle any family quarrels. Only then can they sit down at the holiday feast. The main dish is a stew. The eldest person in the family speaks to the spirits of the dead. Some of the stew is kept for the dead relatives. Their serving is thrown to the vultures, which feed off it. The people believe that the vultures are really the souls of their dead relatives come back to Earth.

24

The end of a church service in Freetown, the captial of Sierra Leone. Africans who are Christians give thanks at their own harvest festivals.

FLOWERS AND GREEN PALMS

Thanksgiving is also a holiday in Cameroon, in Africa. But it has a special African flavour all its own.

Christians in Cameroon celebrate Thanksgiving on September 8. Christians are followers of Jesus Christ. On this day they give thanks for having been told the story of Jesus. Who told them the story? They were told by missionaries, people who spread the teachings of their religion to others. The Christians of Cameroon call their Thanksgiving, *Evamelunga*. This means 'the taking away of the burden of sin'. A sin is any act that is felt to be bad, like telling lies or cheating.

On Thanksgiving morning, churches are decorated with flowers and green palms. Families dress in brightly coloured clothes. A drum beats out an invitation for everyone to come to the meeting in the church. People enter the church singing. During the meeting, people tell why they are grateful. A young boy is grateful because he is now able to read the Bible. A father is glad because his fear of witchcraft has vanished. And all thank God that they have heard the story of Jesus. After the meeting, there is feasting and singing into the night.

25

Celebrating in school

Harvest festivals around the world are a time for singing, dancing and feasting, as well as giving thanks. Families celebrate together at home and in church. Many children celebrate the festival at school, too!

PLAYS AND PARTIES

Putting on a play about Thanksgiving is a good way to learn history, and to have some fun! Teachers and children make costumes. For the Pilgrims, there are bonnets for the women, and

Thanksgiving can be an opportunity to celebrate other historical events – these children are remembering the time America became independent.

hats and shoe buckles for the men. But there is competition to play the part of the American Indians – a favourite role with many in the class.

In some schools, they make a large paper turkey, and each child writes on it to say what they are thankful for. A real turkey has pride of place on the school

Dressed up for the story of the first Thanksgiving.

A church service to celebrate harvest festival

dinner table, and with it, cranberry relish, which the children may have made themselves. It may be sour, or sweetened with orange juice and sugar, or flavoured with walnuts. And everyone leaves room for some delicious apple pie!

GIFTS FOR OTHERS

In Britain, schoolchildren give thanks for the year's harvest at their autumn festival. They may bring gifts of food and flowers that will later be given to people in their community. The gifts are arranged in bright displays, in classrooms or on the stage in the hall. Parents, grandparents and friends may be invited to a special harvest festival assembly, to be entertained with songs and music. Elderly people who live near the school may be given a tea party, or join the children at a church service. Some children may be taken to visit elderly people in their homes, where they sing seasonal songs and present the gifts of food and flowers collected by the school. Classwork might be all about farming, from planting the seeds to harvesting the crops.

Harvest festivals, like many other festivals, are an opportunity to remember the past, and to be thankful for the good things that have happened in the past year.

27

🦃 Let's celebrate! 🦃

JOIN IN THE THANKSGIVING CELEBRATIONS! Try making a turkey table decoration for any special meal, and some delicious cranberry delight to eat with your turkey.

MAKING A PINECONE TURKEY

2 Colour the leaves in bright colours.
3 Cut out the leaves carefully.
4 Set the pine cone on its side. It will be the body of the turkey.
5 Glue the leaves to the bottom of the pine cone to look like feathers. Use the picture on this page to help you.
6 Glue the walnut to the top of the pine cone to make the turkey's head. You might need to snap off a few scales to make the walnut fit.

You will need:
1 a dry pine cone
2 one walnut in its shell
3 coloured card or paper
4 crayons or felt-tip pens
5 PVA glue
6 safe scissors

All you have to do is:
1 Draw six leaf shapes on your card or paper. You could draw round a real leaf to make it easier.

MAKING A CRANBERRY DELIGHT

You will need:
1 1 packet of unflavoured gelatine
2 2 cups of very hot water
3 1 315 gramme jar of cranberry sauce, drained
4 $\frac{1}{2}$ cup chopped walnuts
5 1 cup low-fat sour cream
6 vegetable oil
7 2 large bowls

All you have to do is:
1 Pour the hot water in the bowl and dissolve the gelatine in the water. **Ask an adult** to help with this. Stir in the cranberry sauce.
2 Chill until the cranberry gelatine has slightly thickened.
3 Sir in the nuts. **Warning!** Some people are allergic to nuts. This recipe can be made without nuts.
4 With a spoon, fold the sour cream into the cranberry gelatine.
5 Wipe the inside of a clean bowl with a little vegetable oil, using a piece of kitchen towel. Pour the mixture into the bowl and chill until set. Now enjoy eating your cranberry delight!

29

Glossary

ancient   very old

ancestors   relatives that are long dead

celebrate   to show that a certain day or event is special

celebration   way of celebrating a special day

colonist   a person who settles in a different country

float   a vehicle with a platform that carries an exhibit in a parade

immigrants   people who come to live in a country permanently

Pilgrims   English colonists who settled in Plymouth, Massachusetts, in 1620

soul   the human spirit – the part that is left when the body dies

spirits   beings that you can't see – a bit like ghosts

traditional   customary, an old way of doing something

Index